D1560943

SOLVE THAT CRIME!

# Virtual Crime!

## Solving Cybercrime

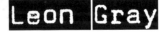

Leon Gray

**Enslow Publishers, Inc.**
40 Industrial Road
Box 398
Berkeley Heights, NJ 07922
USA
   http://www.enslow.com

**Library of Congress Cataloging-in-Publication Data**

Gray, Leon.
  Virtual crime! : solving cybercrime / Leon Gray.
      p. cm. — (Solve that crime!)
  Includes bibliographical references and index.
  Summary: "Shows how forensics helps solve crimes committed on the internet"—Provided by publisher.
  ISBN-13: 978-0-7660-3376-4
  ISBN-10: 0-7660-3376-7
  1. Computer crimes—Investigation—Juvenile literature. 2. Computer crimes—Juvenile literature. I. Title.
  HV8079.C65G73 2009
  363.25'968—dc22

                                    2008033308

Printed in the United States of America

10 9 8 7 6 5 4 3 2 1

**For The Brown Reference Group Ltd.**
Project Editor: Sarah Eason
Designer: Paul Myerscough
Picture Researcher: Maria Joannou
Managing Editor: Miranda Smith
Editorial Director: Lindsey Lowe
Production Director: Alastair Gourlay
Children's Publisher: Anne O'Daly

**Photographic Credits:**
Shutterstock: Lim Yong Hian front cover; Corbis: Serra Antoine 23, Kim Kulish 10, Made Nagi/EPA 18, OutlineLive/Jurgen Frank 19; Dreamstime: Serban Enache 39; Fotolia: Stas Perov 16; Getty Images: Scott Barbour 32, Glenn Chapman/AFP 17; Istockphoto: 37, 43, Lise Gagne 24, Ed Hidden 6, Stefan Klein 15, Perry Kroll 35, Rich Legg 7, 38, Felix Möckel 29, Andreas Reh 5, Jamie Wilson 26; Photoshot: Zoriah/WpN 8; Rex Features: Tamara Beckwith 40, Sipa Press 21; Shutterstock: Kharidehal Abhirama Ashwin 20, Yury Asotov 44, Franck Boston 4, Jack Dagley Photography 14, Zhu Difeng 30, Romanchuck Dimitry 12, Junial Enterprises 34, Ramzi Hachicho 9, Lim Yong Hian 28, MDD 27, Monkey Business Images 36, Kheng Guan Toh 13, Vatikaki 11.

# Contents

# What is cybercrime?

**P**eople spend more time on computers and the internet than ever before—shopping, chatting, making new friends, and studying and working online. Some people have seen this as a way to commit a new type of crime, called cybercrime.

Personal computers (PCs) have only been around for a few decades. The first was the Altair 8800, which came onto the market in 1974. Three years later, Apple Computer released the Apple II. The Apple II was cheap and easy to use. It started a computer revolution. Apple's main competitor was the IBM PC, which ran on Microsoft programs. Today, most PCs are based on the IBM or Apple design. Many people use them at home, at school, and at work.

## The Internet

The internet developed from a computer network linking businesses, the military, and universities in the US. The network, called Arpanet, grew in a huge community of computer users.

*Many criminals commit their crimes in the virtual world of computers and the internet.*

Gradually, computers users around the world joined the network. Arpanet became the internet.

In 1990, a computer expert from England, named Tim Berners-Lee, invented the World Wide Web (www). This enabled people to find and retrieve information on the internet. Surfing the internet and sending e-mails has since become an everyday part of life for most people.

## Cybercrime
As quickly as computers and the internet have revolutionized our lives, criminals have developed new ways of carrying out their crimes. Cybercrime is any type of crime that involves using computers and the internet. It includes crimes such as identity theft and hacking. Forensic scientists have risen to the challenge of solving these cybercrimes.

5

*Forensic scientists examine a computer to reveal evidence of criminal activities.*

## Fighting cybercrime
Many people think that cybercrime is spiraling out of control. In 2007, cybercrime cost the American economy $117 billion. In Great Britain, computer crime occurs every ten seconds. This adds up to 3.1 million crimes each year— far more than the number of crimes taking place on the streets. Computer crimes are probably much more widespread, because people do not always report them.

Many countries now have squads of cybercops. These dedicated police workers trawl the internet to fight cybercrime. The police and forensic scientists put the cybercriminals behind bars.

# Different cybercrimes

**C**ybercrime is a new type of crime that takes place in the virtual world of computers, telephones, and the internet. It is one of the fastest-growing areas of crime thanks to the rapid spread of the World Wide Web.

People use computers and the internet to commit many different types of crimes.

- Cybercrime can include hacking. This is when people use computers to break into other computer systems without the owners knowing about it.

*Criminals can steal passwords and other personal information by watching people using computers in airports and other public places.*

*A computer contains a record of the criminal's activities, so it is vital evidence in cases of cybercrime.*

7

- Some criminals launder money on the internet. This means they buy products and services on the internet using money obtained from their crimes.
- Cybercrime also includes traditional crimes such as fraud. Crooks use fake web sites and other scams to steal money or private information such as credit card details.
- Many people are breaking the law without even realizing it when they share music files, movies, and computer programs with other internet users.
- High-profile cybercrimes include child pornography, fraud, the selling and purchase of illegal guns or drugs, or other material that are protected by copyright.
- Cyberterrorism includes terrorist attacks against government computers, such as hacking into computers belonging to the military. Terrorists also use the internet to post instructions for terrorist attacks in chat rooms and on bulletin boards.

## TRUE CRIME...

### First cyberterrorism

In the late 1980s, a group of German hackers hit the headlines when they were arrested for breaking into US military computers. In a case dubbed "The Cuckoo's Egg," it was revealed that the hackers stole passwords, computer programs, and other secret information from the computers and sold it to the KGB—the security services of the former Soviet Union. The hackers were eventually found guilty of espionage (spying).

## IN DEPTH

# Identity theft

One of the fastest growing cybercrimes is identity theft. Every year, more than nine million Americans are victims of this type of crime. Crooks persuade people to reveal personal information such as addresses, birth dates, credit card details, and passwords to bank accounts. High tech criminals use the internet to get this information by sending e-mails pretending to be a bank or some other well known company. This is called "phishing." They may then use the information to get a passport or apply for a bank loan and steal thousands of dollars. Often, the victim will only find out when the bank contacts them.

*Some criminals get personal information by searching through household trash for items such as checks and credit card receipts.*

## Tool or target

The computer is central to every cybercrime. The computer may be either the tool or the target of the crime. Spamming is one example of using a computer as a tool in crimes. Spamming involves using computers to send junk e-mail to people who have not asked for it. Spamming itself may not be a crime, but many crooks are now using spam to commit crimes such as fraud.

Sometimes the computer is the target of a crime. Viruses and worms are computer programs that spread around the internet from one computer to millions of other computers. Some people develop viruses and worms as jokes. These programs may not be harmful themselves, but they still cause problems by jamming the internet.

Other viruses and worms are more harmful because they damage computers or delete important files. Some viruses and worms take control of computers. Criminals then use these computers to commit other crimes, such as sending spam to commit fraud or distribute pornographic images.

## Internet and the law

The internet does not recognize the borders between countries, so it is easy for criminals to carry out their illegal activities far from the scene of their crimes. An investigation that begins in one country can quickly lead to another. It is hard to convict the criminals unless the two countries work together to track them down. Different countries also have different laws. Some activities may be a crime in one country but not in another. As a result, it is difficult to stop some types of cybercrime.

*Some criminals use computers to coordinate terrorist activities such as bombings. This is known as cyberterrorism.*

9

# Computer forensics

When someone uses a computer to commit a crime, the computer stores the information about his or her activities. High tech criminals try to hide the crime trail, but experts can often recover the hidden information. This evidence can help convict the criminal in court.

Computer forensics includes the recovery of information stored on any type of electronic device, from personal computers, cell phones, and personal digital assistants to fax machines, servers, and GPS (global positioning system) navigation devices.

The experts who find the hidden evidence are called forensic examiners. What they recover depends on the crimes involved.

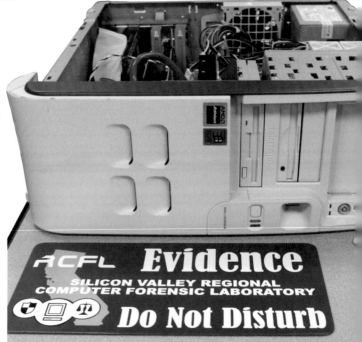

*Computer forensics is becoming very important as more criminals turn to cybercrime.*

RCFL **Evidence**
SILICON VALLEY REGIONAL
COMPUTER FORENSIC LABORATORY
**Do Not Disturb**

The hard drive is a permanent record of a criminal's activities.

## IN THE LAB

## Chain of evidence

The main aim of a computer forensics examination is to gather evidence for use in court. Similar to any forensic examination, the examiner must follow guidelines to record the chain of evidence. Imagine that detectives find a computer at a suspect's house. After isolating the computer to ensure that it cannot be tampered with, the examiner will make a copy of the hard drive. The original hard drive will then be locked away for safety. The examiner will do a wide range of forensic tests on the copy. They will search for hidden, damaged, or deleted files and try to decipher files that are encrypted. All the evidence is then carefully written down in a report that can be read out in court.

The evidence found could be a text message on a cell phone. This might place a suspect at the crime scene, or prove that he or she could not have been there. The information could be cash records for crimes such as the sale of illegal drugs. A computer can be used to store illegal copies of music files or distribute pornographic images. Forensic examiners might find evidence of hacking. The list is endless.

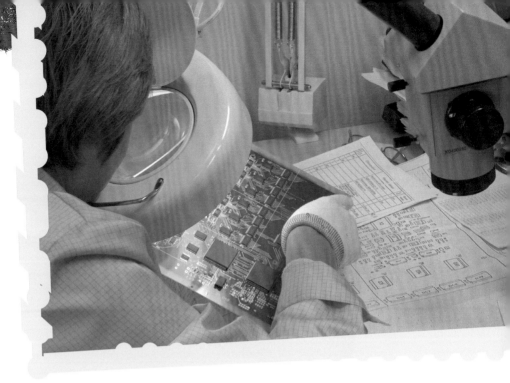

## Solving crimes

Computers help detectives solve crimes in many other ways. Virtual reality can be used to reconstruct crime scenes from photographs. Computer analysis can help identify a person on a criminal database. For example, results from fingerprint samples can be compared to records held on a database.

*A forensic expert examines a circuit board taken from a computer to reveal information that can be used as evidence in court.*

## IN THE LAB

### Tracing calls

Computers are not the only digital devices that may record criminal activities. Cell phones store text messages, lists of calls made and received, and address books of contacts. Forensic examiners can retrieve all of this data and even more. Call location analysis is a forensic examination that can help pinpoint where a person was when he or she made or received a call or text message. Forensic examiners can use call location analysis to confirm whether or not a suspect was near a crime scene at the time of the crime.

## Forensics at work

Computer forensics can be useful for purposes other than solving crimes. For example, American workers spend around six hours a week surfing the internet for personal use. This time spent "cyberslacking" costs employers $178 billion every year. Companies are now hiring forensic examiners to monitor internet use at work. These investigations may reveal more serious cases of internet abuse, such as employees who are downloading illegal material from web sites.

## IN DEPTH

## International criminal database

Many countries store information about criminals and suspects in computer databases. Useful details include photographs, false names, and past convictions. Many databases also include biometric data, such as fingerprints and iris (eye) scans, that are unique to each person. Police use these databases to find matches with evidence collected from crime scenes. Since many crimes now cross international borders, some people think that countries should cooperate and share the information held on their databases. Others are concerned about personal privacy. They think that it will be hard to keep the information held on an international database safe.

13

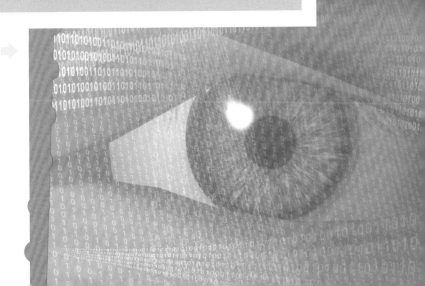

*Iris scans and other biometric data are stored on databases to help the police identify criminals.*

# Virtual crime scenes

I t is 9:00 AM on a Saturday morning. The parking lot is starting to fill up with weekend shoppers. A murder victim is lying on the ground, with wounds on his head and his neck. There are bloodstains on his ripped clothes and dents on the hood of his car.

14

Most crimes happen in areas where a lot of people move around and would disturb the evidence. When the forensic team arrives at a murder scene they need to act quickly. Once the crime scene is secure, forensic examiners measure the dimensions of the area involved and record the position of the body and blood splatter markings.

*Police secure the crime scene before forensic scientists begin to collect any evidence.*

Photographers capture every angle on camera to record the crime scene.

## Virtual reality graphics

Back at the crime lab, forensic examiners use computers to interpret the evidence at crime scenes. Photogrammetry is a technique in which computers combine hundreds of photos taken by special cameras into a 360-degree image. Using virtual reality (VR), people can move through the virtual crime scene by clicking on a mouse. It is as if they were really there. They also have the advantage of looking at the crime scene from any angle.

15

## Preserving the evidence

In the real world, forensic experts have only a limited time to examine the crime scene. But they can revisit a virtual reality crime scene as many times as they want to. Virtual reality crime scenes also help forensic teams test various theories or check out witness statements. For example, a forensic examiner can view the crime scene as if he or she was actually there and use this inside knowledge to test witness statements.

## EXAMINE THE EVIDENCE

### Fact or fiction?

Virtual reality has made it easier for juries to see crime scene evidence. All they need to do is to look on a computer screen to see the virtual crime scene. But critics think that evidence shown in virtual reality crime scenes is so good that it may fool people into believing things that did not really happen.

# Hacking

**H**acking means breaking into a computer system. The people who do this are called hackers or crackers. Some hackers break into computers to commit crimes. Other hackers do it for fun or to highlight problems with computer security.

The first hackers appeared in the 1970s, but they did not break into computers. These early hackers targeted telephone systems and made calls for free. In the 1980s, these phone hackers, or "phreaks" as they were known, started to hack into computers. Then the hackers started to share tips on bulletin boards, and hacking became more sophisticated. The problem became much worse when the internet became public during the 1990s.

16

Criminal hackers cripple computer systems around the world and cause billions of dollars worth of damage every year.

## White Hats

Many big businesses employ experts to hack into their computer systems on purpose. This so-called ethical hacking helps companies improve the security of their computers. Hackers who help companies secure their computer systems are called "white hats."

*Hackers share tips at a sponsored "Hack Day" at the Yahoo! headquarters in California.*

## Who are the hackers?

Hackers who break into computer systems to commit crimes are called "black hats." Some black hats delete files and damage computers in simple acts of vandalism. Others steal information and make money by selling it to other criminals. Expert hackers break directly into banks and big businesses to steal the money.

Hackers called "hacktivists" break into government or company web sites to put across their point of view. For example, animal-rights activists might deface the web sites of companies that test their products on animals. Most hacktivists think that hacktivism is nothing more than free speech. Others are criminals who set out to cause as much damage as possible.

## IN DEPTH
## Ports

Information passes in and out of a computer through channels called ports. A PC has more than 65,000 ports to exchange information with other computers. Hackers often sneak into computers through one of the ports without the user noticing.

## IN DEPTH

### Chaos computer club

The Chaos Computer Club (CCC) is a group of hackers from Germany. Founded in 1981, the CCC is one of the oldest hacking communities. The club first hit the headlines in 1989, when hackers from the group were arrested for spying for the Soviet KGB. Today, the CCC is better known for hactivism. The group argues for freedom of information and free computer access for all. Hackers from the group have revealed security flaws in Microsoft software and problems with computers that count votes during elections.

Many hackers break into computer systems for fun. These so-called "recreational hackers" enjoy the challenge of breaking into the computer systems of governments and big businesses. Some do it to highlight weaknesses in computer security. They argue that hacking helps to increase security.

*Many recreational hackers go to seminars and workshops where they learn new skills.*

*Kevin Mitnick has turned his obsession with hacking into a full-time job.*

## TRUE CRIME...

### Master Hacker

Kevin Mitnick was once America's most wanted hacker. His first arrest came in 1989 after hacking into the computer system of Digital Equipment Corporation and stealing $1 million worth of software. Mitnick pleaded guilty and spent a year in jail. After his release, Mitnick got a job as a computer programmer, but his obsession with hacking prompted the FBI to issue a warrant for his arrest in 1992. Mitnick went on the run, but even as a fugitive he continued to hack into the computers of big businesses such as Motorola and Nokia. The FBI eventually traced Mitnick in 1995 with the help of a computer expert named Tsutomu Shimomura. Mitnick was sent to jail for five years. He was released in 2000 and now runs a company that helps businesses to stop hackers from breaking into their computers.

## Following a trail

Most hackers are computer experts who are good at hiding their crimes, but they do leave telltale signs. These clues can be used to track them down. Some computer programs can find out the IP (Internet Protocol) address of a hacker. Every computer that is connected to the internet has a unique IP address, which is a sequence of numbers. A clever forensic examiner can trace the IP address to a particular street in a city or town. Although catching hackers by locating their IP addresses sounds easy, hackers usually break into distant computers that are not their own and then do all their hacking from there. An examiner often has to follow a long trail of hacked computers before reaching the source of the crime. Often, the hacker will have already moved on.

# Electronic infection

**I**n the past, people spread "malware" (malicious software) using floppy disks. Today, the internet is flooded with programs designed to damage computers. Electronic infection is a major problem for all computer users.

Malware can stop computers from working properly and causes billions of dollars worth of damage and lost work time. The most common forms of malware are viruses, e-mail viruses, worms, and Trojan horses (programs that appear to be useful but secretly damage computer systems).

*Floppy disks were used to spread the first worms and viruses.*

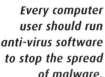

*Every computer user should run anti-virus software to stop the spread of malware.*

- Viruses are programs that run alongside normal programs such as Microsoft Word or Internet Explorer. The virus spreads to other computers whenever the user runs the program.
- Some viruses target e-mail programs such as Outlook Express. These viruses spread by sending e-mails to people listed in the e-mail address book.
- Worms infect computers by scanning them for security holes. The worm sends a copy of itself through the hole and then starts scanning for security holes in other computers.
- Trojan horses appear to do one thing but actually do something completely different. Trojan horses cannot spread in the same way as viruses and worms, but they can do a lot of damage if they get onto computer systems.

## TRUE CRIME...

### Morris Worm

The Morris Worm was one of the first worms to spread on the internet. A student named Robert Morris from Cornell University wrote the worm. He released it in November 1988 from computers at the Massachusetts Institute of Technology, because he was trying to hide the fact he was a student from Cornell. Morris wrote the code for the worm to figure out how big the internet was, but he made a mistake. The worm spread through the internet much too quickly. Thousands of computers at universities, government web sites, and research facilities ground to a halt. Morris was convicted, but he did not go to jail. He received a suspended sentence with community service and was fined $10,000. Morris now works as an associate professor at the Massachusetts Institute of Technology.

## Other threats

Spyware is malware that hides on computers and gathers private information such as surfing history. Spyware authors sell this information to companies that use it to advertise their products. Spyware often comes bundled with adware. This type of malware displays unwanted pop-up windows. The pop-ups advertise products the spyware thinks you might like to buy based on your surfing habits.

A more sinister form of spyware can log the keystrokes on the keyboard and can even take snapshots of the computer screen. In the worst cases, this information can be used to commit crimes such as identity theft and fraud by recording credit card details, passwords, and other personal information.

## Preventing malware

Anti-virus software and firewalls are tools that help people protect computers from malware such as worms and viruses. Anti-virus software scans all the files on a computer's hard disk. If the software detects a virus, it will remove it or make it harmless.

## IN DEPTH

# How worms and viruses spread

Most computer users have heard of viruses and worms. But many people still do not understand the difference between them. A virus infects a computer and causes it, when prompted, to spread to other computers. Viruses usually contain extra instructions that may cause other problems, such as deleting or damaging files. Worms can do the same damage as viruses but they can spread to other computers without prompting. Like viruses, worms usually contain instructions that cause additional problems. So viruses depend on a computer user to do something, such as open an e-mail attachment or click on a link, to help them spread, while worms can spread by themselves.

As people write new virus programs, computer experts write new programs, called signatures, that help them identify the viruses. Anti-virus software downloads new signatures as soon as they are written so that new viruses can be stopped. Every computer user should run anti-virus software every day.

A firewall is a computer program that controls the information entering and leaving a computer. Most firewalls control the flow of information through ports. If a worm or virus is targeting a particular port that a firewall has closed, then the malware cannot infect the computer system.

## TRUE CRIME...

### Melissa

Melissa is the name of a computer virus that first appeared in March 1999. Computers became infected when users opened up a Microsoft Word document attached to e-mails. The virus contained instructions to grab the first 50 names from the user's e-mail address book and resend itself to those e-mail addresses. In a matter of hours, Melissa spread throughout computer systems around the world. The virus created huge volumes of e-mail and cost businesses millions of dollars. Less then a week after Melissa appeared, forensic experts traced the source of the virus to David Smith from New Jersey. Smith spent 20 months in jail for his crime.

23

*The Melissa virus flooded the internet with e-mail when Smith released it in March 1999.*

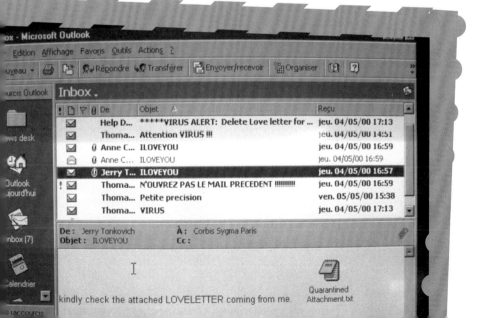

# Internet fraud

**A**nyone who uses the internet to send e-mail or instant messages, visit chat rooms, or surf the Web is at risk from fraud. There are many different types of internet fraud, but they are all designed to con people out of their money.

The internet is like a global shopping mall. But it is often hard to tell the difference between an honest trader and a crook on the internet. Some crooks trick people into handing over private information, such as bank account or credit card numbers. They use these details to buy goods and services. There are also criminals who lure people by inviting them to take part in get-rich-quick and investment schemes.

*Credit cards are an easy way to pay for goods. But criminals are also finding it easy to commit fraud with someone else's credit card details.*

## Retail fraud

Many crooks set up bogus internet companies that pretend to sell valuable goods at bargain prices. Unsuspecting shoppers enter their credit card details online, the web site disappears, and the goods never arrive. By the time a victim realizes what has happened, the crooks have run up huge debts on the victim's credit card. Variations on this scam occur on auction web sites such as eBay. Dishonest sellers offer genuine goods in an auction, but ship fake or stolen items to the winning bidder—or the goods never arrive.

 *Look for the secure site padlock symbol to protect yourself from internet fraud.*

## Phishing

Crooks often use a scam called "phishing" to trick people out of their money. The criminals send e-mails pretending to come from a bank or some other well known company. The e-mail might contain a web link that directs to a web page that looks almost identical to the genuine web page. The web site will invite the person to key in personal details.

## IN DEPTH

### Vishing

Criminals are coming up with new scams to fool people into handing over personal details. One of these is called "vishing" or "voice phishing." This scam is a variation on phishing. Instead of using bogus Web sites, vishing uses telephones to trick people into handing over their details.

How does it work? The first step comes in the form of a text message that warns people that something is wrong with their bank account or credit card. The message asks the person to call a number to verify their account. On the phone, an automated message asks the victim to reveal all the account information, such as the card number, expiration date, birth date, and other personal information. Many people do so because they trust telephones more than the internet.

25

People who do not trust ➡
the internet can still fall
victim to "vishing" scams.

## TRUE CRIME...

### The Big Phish

In 2005, police in Brazil arrested Valdir
Paulo de Almeida—the head of one
of the world's biggest phishing gangs.
Every day for two years, the gang sent
bogus messages to around three million
e-mail accounts. A Trojan horse attached
to the e-mail included spyware that
recorded the keys people pressed on
their keyboards. This fed account user
names and passwords back to the gang.
In just two years, the gang collected
$37 million from online bank accounts
in Brazil and abroad. Forensic examiners
eventually managed to follow the
electronic trail back to the gang.

26

This could be the bank account number or a password. This
gives the criminal access to the victim's real bank account.
This type of fraud is usually easy to spot. Genuine banks and
companies will never ask someone to reveal a password on
an account. The e-mails banks and companies send almost
always contain personal information, such as part of an
account number. Even so, millions of people fall victim
to phishing every year at a cost of billions of dollars.

## Get-rich-quick schemes

Sounds too good to be true? It probably is. But people still fall
victims to get-rich-quick schemes on the internet. In the Lottery
scam, crooks send e-mails telling people they have won prizes.
The e-mail asks the "winner" to call a premium-rate number

(at huge cost) or send money to claim the prize. Other scams invite people to learn about amazing business opportunities that guarantee thousands of dollars of earnings a month. Some people pay to find out more, but the information never arrives.

## Investment fraud

Many criminals use the internet to make money on the stock market. The crooks send e-mails to spread false information about stocks and shares, or post the news on message boards and in chat rooms. Spreading rumors about a company can make the price of its stock rise or fall dramatically. Criminals make money buying stocks and shares when the price is low and then selling them when the price is high. Telling lies about a company to influence the price of its stock is a serious crime in most countries.

## IN DEPTH

### Pharming

Pharming is another phishing variation. Unlike phishing, which directs the victim to a bogus web site using an e-mail as "bait," pharming redirects the victim to a bogus web site even if the correct web address is keyed in. Hackers do this by breaking into the computers that direct internet traffic. The internet browser shows the correct Web site, which makes pharming even harder to detect.

*Criminals use the internet to manipulate the price of stocks and shares.*

27

# Spamming

Everyone who has an e-mail account receives lots of junk e-mail messages called spam. People who send spam e-mail are called spammers. Some spammers send e-mails advertising perfectly legal products. Other spammers are crooks.

What annoys people about spam advertising products is the sheer volume that floods the internet. Spam is easy and cheap to send. Spammers send as much of it as they can to make as much money as they can. Crooks also use spam to con people out of money. And they use it to send viruses and worms as well as to direct people to pornographic web sites.

Spammers get e-mail addresses in many ways. The companies that provide e-mail accounts, called e-mail hosts, are the biggest targets. The hosts hold lists of e-mail accounts, and their computers are open to attack by hackers. Another source for spammers is the internet—chat rooms, newsgroups, and web sites.

◀ Spam filters remove junk e-mail before it reaches the Inbox.

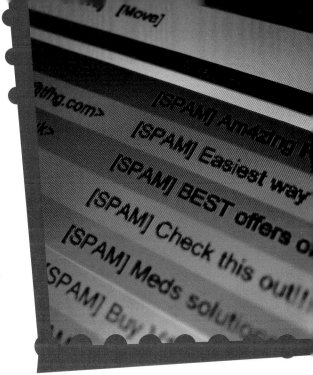

*Receiving huge amounts of spam every day can cause people stress.*

Programs called spambots trawl the internet looking for an "@" symbol that forms part of an e-mail address. Many companies ask their customers for their e-mail addresses and then sell them to spammers. Once the spammers have the addresses, they share them with other spammers.

## Stopping spam

The best way to reduce the amount of spam you get is to use a spam filter. The filter removes junk e-mail before it reaches the recipient. Even the best filters let some spam through. Sometimes they delete e-mail messages that you want to receive. Another step is to ignore spam. Some spam includes web links where it appears that people can choose to no longer receive the spam by "unsubscribing." This is a trick. More spam is likely to arrive by clicking this web link. The spammer then knows the e-mail address is active.

Many companies avoid spam by using alternatives, such as online forms, to communicate with their customers. Some countries have introduced laws to try and stop the spammers.

## TRUE CRIME...

### Robert Soloway

Nicknamed the "Spam King," Robert Alan Soloway was once one of the top ten internet spammers in the world. Soloway infected computers with viruses and then used them to send out millions of junk e-mails advertising his services. Soloway used his spam to launder money and commit identity theft and fraud. He stole millions of dollars from his victims. In 2008, he was sentenced to 47 months in prison for his crimes.

# Zombie computers

**S**ome hackers are secretly breaking into the computers of people from around the world and using them to carry out their crimes. In some cases, one hacker might control millions of these so-called "zombie computers." They use them to send out spam or flood web sites with e-mails.

Most people do not know their computers have been taken over by a hacker. Their computers might be much slower than normal, but otherwise they work perfectly well. The first time a computer user might find out he or she has been the victim of an attack is when the Internet Service Provider (ISP) cancels the service.

◄ *Most hackers use malware to set up zombie networks.*

# Infection

Hackers use e-mails, web sites, and many other tools to recruit zombie computers. For example, a pop-up window on a web site might invite you to click on a web link. In fact, by clicking on the link you are downloading a file that contains a worm or virus. The hacker is one step closer to enlisting another zombie computer.

## IN DEPTH

### What's in a name?

Spammers target other forms of internet communication as well as e-mail. Spim is identical to spam, but it appears on all instant messengers (IM) such as AOL Instant Messenger. Many instant messengers list users and include personal information about their age and sex. This makes it easy for spammers to target their advertisements.

## Activation

Once the malware has been installed, the computer user has to activate it. Hackers design malware to look like picture files or some other normal file format. When the user clicks on the file to see the information he or she has downloaded, this activates the worm or virus. The computer is now a zombie computer. Every time the user switches his or her computer on, the hacker can use it to commit their crimes.

31

## Zombie networks

Most hackers use their network of zombie computers to send spam. Hackers can send millions of spam messages every day with a large zombie network. Some companies pay hackers to advertise their products using spam e-mail. Other hackers use spam to distribute malware, or send phishing messages to trick people into revealing private information. Another use of zombie networks is distributed denial-of-service (DOS) attacks. In this case, the hacker uses the network of zombie computers to attack a web site by flooding it with thousands of e-mails at the same time. The sudden increase in internet traffic slows down the web site. This type of activity may even shut the site down completely.

# Company cybercrime

**B**anks and big businesses face a growing threat from cybercrime. Some criminals steal money directly by hacking into computer systems. Others steal ideas about new products and use them to get money by threatening to sell them to a rival company. This serious crime is called blackmail.

*Computers at the London offices of Japanese bank Sumitomo Mitsui came under attack on March 17, 2005.*

## TRUE CRIME...

### The Japanese job

In 2004, a gang of crooks targeted the Japanese bank Sumitomo Mitsui in one of the world's biggest attempted online bank robberies. The gang hacked into the bank's computer system and tried to transfer more than $420 million. The bank raid failed when one of the gang was caught moving $26 million into an Israeli bank account.

TEMPLE COURT

SMBC SUMITOMO MITSUI BANKING CORPORATION

LEGAL & GENERAL

It takes great skill to break into a bank. These organizations spend huge amounts of money on high tech computer security. But a growing number of attacks are by people on the inside—workers who are motivated by greed or may bear a grudge. Organized gangs plant people in companies to steal data and assist outside attacks. Hacking attempts on banks and other big companies could not take place without the help of someone on the inside.

## Revenge attacks

Revenge plays a part in many cybercrimes. Unhappy customers or ex-workers might hack into the company's computers and delete important files. Or they might use malware to damage computer systems. Programs called logic bombs run after a certain date or period of time. When triggered, the logic bomb explodes and deletes files or damages data. People who write computer programs often hide logic bombs in their software. They can trigger a logic bomb at any time, for example, if they lose their job.

33

## Hacktivism

People often hack into computer systems as a form of protest. These "hacktivists" often alter the content of the web sites to make their views heard. In more serious cases, hacktivists flood web sites with spam as part of a distributed denial-of-service attack. This type of attack costs companies a lot of money.

## IN DEPTH

### Data encryption

Companies use data encryption to protect the information they hold on their computers. Data encryption involves jumbling up data using complex computer programs. Scrambled data cannot be read by anyone until it is unscrambled using a "key." This ensures sensitive information stays out of unwanted hands.

# Pirates on the Net

**P**iracy is big business. Criminal gangs make billions of dollars every year selling illegal copies of music, movies, and software. Everyday computer users are adding to the problem by sharing the pirate copies on the internet.

"Piracy" is the word used to describe the sale of illegal copies of computer games, movies, and music. In most countries, copyright law protects the work of artists such as musicians and moviemakers. This means people cannot copy anything unless they have permission to do so. However, criminals sell pirate copies in markets and online auction web sites. Many people buy them because they cost much less than the genuine items even though the quality can be poor. Movies may be grainy because they may have been downloaded from the internet or recorded on a camcorder at the back of a movie theater.

## Downloading files

Downloading music from the internet is now more popular than buying CDs from a store.

*Downloading music files from the internet without paying for them is against the law.*

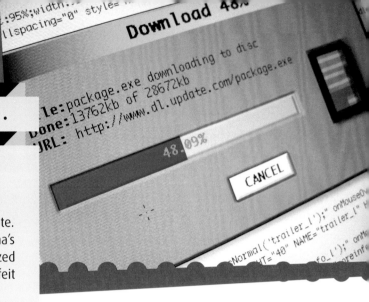

## Chinese pirates

In 2007, the FBI and Chinese police smashed one of the biggest-ever piracy rings to date. During a series of raids in China's Guangdong Province, they seized about $500 million of counterfeit Microsoft programs. Microsoft Corporation helped the FBI track down the pirates. It developed a scheme to identify fake copies during software updates. The scheme showed that Chinese copies were being used in 27 countries worldwide, costing Microsoft around $2 billion.

*Scan any files you download to check that they are free from malware such as viruses or worms.*

Many different web sites sell albums legally. A web site may charge a fee for each download or a fee to download a certain number of tracks every month. They may offer free downloads, too. Other web sites allow people to share files. These peer-to-peer (P2P) networks can be used to share photos or video clips that people have taken themselves. But most P2P networks are full of pirated music and movies that people can download for free. When people share these files they are breaking the law.

## EXAMINE THE EVIDENCE 35

### Share safely

* Keep your personal information private. Criminals can use it to commit fraud.
* Run the most up-to-date security software before downloading files from P2P networks. Criminals use P2P networks to distribute malware.
* Use security features built into P2P networks as well as your own security software. Most have anti-spyware tools, firewalls, and secure file-sharing systems.
* Never download music without paying for it. It is against the law to share music that is protected by copyright.

# Obscenity on the Net

Anyone can stumble across obscene material on the internet. There are millions of web sites that show pornographic photos and videos. Some people actively look for this material. Criminals also use spam e-mails to direct people to their sites.

The laws governing obscenity are hard to enforce, because it is very difficult to say what is obscene. One person may find a photograph perfectly acceptable, but another person may find it extremely offensive. There are so many web sites that show obscene material that it is impossible to monitor every one. In most countries, however, there are laws that aim to protect children from obscene material.

## Tackling obscenity

Different countries are working together to help stamp out obscenity on the internet. The police takes the threat very seriously. In many countries, there are dedicated teams of cybercops who scour chat rooms and newsgroups looking for criminals who post obscene material on the internet.

◄ *As long as you are careful, you can safely meet friends in chat rooms and talk using e-mail.*

*Using a webcam is fun if the person you are talking to is genuine.*

Customer : Hello

Advisor: Good afternoon how can I help ...

Customer: I have a problem with ........

Customer Details

Gender: Female
Name: Mrs Smith

Operating System: Yes
Current Customer: Yes

## IN DEPTH

## Face value

It is important to remember that people are not necessarily who they say they are when you meet them on the internet. While it is fine to chat and send e-mails to people you know and trust, such as family and friends, you need to be careful when you meet new friends online. Some people might seem to be friendly at first. If they start making inappropriate suggestions, however, tell an adult who you can trust immediately.

## Added problems

Anyone who looks at obscene web sites can expect to have trouble with malware such as spyware, Trojan horses, viruses, and worms. They can also expect to receive a lot of spam e-mail directing them to more obscene web sites. Sometimes it is hard to get away from the web sites altogether. As soon as you click off a web site, a new obscene web site pops up in another window. The best way to stop this from happening is to avoid obscene material on the internet completely.

## EXAMINE THE EVIDENCE

### Chat room checklist

* Never give out personal information such as your real name or address in an internet chat room.
* Never arrange to meet someone who you know only from the internet. Remember that people may not always be the person they claim they are.
* If you are worried about anyone you have met on the internet tell someone you can trust.

# Bad behavior

**M**any young internet users are victims of cyberbullying. All too often the bullies treat their behavior as a joke, but threatening people and writing lies about them is wrong. In some cases, the bullies may be breaking the law.

Online bullying, called cyberbullying, is a big problem among young internet users. Bullies use e-mail, instant messages, chat rooms, blogs, and web sites to send lies and hurtful messages about people. Bullies sometimes trick people into revealing embarrassing information and then send it to others. Sometimes they post pictures of their victims on the internet without the victims knowing. Some bullies hack into their victim's e-mail and send cruel messages while pretending to be that person. Or they might create web sites or blogs and poke fun at the victim.

## Cyberstalking

Another type of harassment is called cyberstalking. It occurs when someone sends nasty e-mails, instant messages, text messages by cell phone, and posts in news groups and chat rooms.

*Sending hurtful messages by text message is a common form of cyberbullying.*

*Cyberstalking can be a big problem, so report it to the Internet Service Provider immediately.*

Cyberstalking involves repeated threats. In some cases, it develops from an argument in the real world. More serious cases of cyberstalking involve threats that spill into the real world. These may develop into serious physical attacks.

## Stop the cyberstalkers

There are a few simple steps people can take to avoid becoming the victim of a cyberstalker. Many people choose a false name when they are online. They use it to set up an e-mail account. They keep their main e-mail account to send messages to people they know and trust. They use the second account for everything else. It is important to use the filters that come with e-mail programs. Spam filters block junk e-mail, but there are other filters that can be used to block messages from particular addresses.

## EXAMINE THE EVIDENCE

### Stop the bullies

If you or anyone else you know is a victim of cyberbullying, there are a few simple steps you can take to stop it.

- Do not forward hurtful messages from cyberbullies.
- Exclude bullies from your buddy list, and block their e-mail addresses.
- Report cyberbullying to someone you can trust, such as a family member or friend.

# A global problem

Criminal gangs are working on a scale much bigger than ever before. They often live in one country and use the internet to break the law in another. Governments are also fighting electronic wars using the internet. Many spy on the computer systems of other countries and disrupt their web sites so they do not work properly.

One of the biggest problems is the drug industry. Thanks to the internet, people can buy drugs that they would normally only get from a doctor. Buying drugs in this way is dangerous because people can never be sure what they are taking. Many of these drugs contain harmful substances.

Some crooks sell illegal drugs on the internet, too. They set up drug deals using e-mail or instant messages and meet at internet cafés to do the deals. Criminals also meet up in restricted-access chat rooms to buy and sell instructions to make illegal drugs such as methamphetamine.

*The terrorist attack on the World Trade Center in 2001 was planned and coordinated using computers.*

## Cyberwarfare

When people think of war, they usually imagine soldiers fighting with bombs and bullets. The internet has made a new type of warfare possible—"cyberwarfare"—where computers are used as the weapons.

Cyberwarfare includes distributed denial-of-service attacks, when one country floods Web sites in another with so much information that they crash. It also includes spying, when computers are used to intercept and decipher secret messages. In some cases, hackers try to break into military computers or attack essential services such as banks and water supplies.

## Real threat

In 2007, computers in China were used to hack into the Pentagon, as well as computers in Britain, France, and Germany. China denies the attack. In 2007, another attack occurred in Estonia. Banks, media, and even the Estonian parliament were all targeted. Officials blamed Russia, but it denied the attack. The US government is planning to spend billions of dollars to tackle cyberwarfare. The military is also developing software to tackle the threats, and using normal counterintelligence measures to assess the level of risk.

## IN DEPTH: Terrorists on the Net

Terrorists fight their campaigns on the internet as well as the real world. There are hundreds of web sites supporting terrorist groups. Terrorists use the internet in many different ways. They spread fear by showing images of their atrocities or posting messages threatening to carry out attacks. The internet also provides terrorists with a voice—they can spread their beliefs, raise funds, speak with others, and recruit new people to the cause. They also surf the internet as a source of information, for example, about how to build bombs. Sometimes terrorists plan their attacks as coded messages in chat rooms and by e-mail.

41

# Staying safe

There are many ways to avoid becoming the next victim of a cybercrime. Everyone should keep personal information private. Do not give out account details or passwords to anyone on the internet. Some people also protect their identity by using false names for e-mail accounts and chat rooms.

When a cybercrime occurs, do not let the crooks get away with it. Many people do not report cybercrimes because they are embarrassed. It is important to report any cybercrimes involving computers to the police and your ISP. This may stop someone else from becoming a victim.

*Your browser will show a padlock symbol if it is safe to log in to the web site.*

## Safe shopping

Shopping online is not like visiting a shopping mall. In the real world, people talk to a sales assistant and see what they are buying before handing over the money. How can anyone be sure that an online store is real?

One thing to look out for are contact details for the site.

Avoid web sites that do not include a real contact address and telephone number. Online web sites such as Amazon and eBay are safer than most because they use seller-rating systems. The seller rating is a score given by buyers who have dealt with the seller before. Some web sites use a secure site padlock symbol to show that they are protected and therefore safe to use.

## WiFi

Many people use WiFi to connect to the internet. WiFi connections do not need wires; the computer connects to the internet using radio signals. It is vital to protect your WiFi connection with a secure password. If you do not, people can use it for free.

43

*WiFi makes it easy to surf the web from anywhere but be sure you protect the connection with a password.*

# Forensics in the field

**I**nterested in a career as a cybercrime fighter? You will need expert knowledge of computers and the internet. A degree in computer science is also highly desirable.

Computer forensics is one of the latest developments in the fight against cybercrime. Scientists in this field can expect to work on a range of crimes, such as identity theft, internet fraud, and terrorist threats. They use the latest techniques to examine computers involved in crimes.

*Forensic computer examiners have a detailed knowledge of how computers work.*

## SALARY CHART

This chart shows how much some forensic scientists working in the field of computer forensics can expect to earn.

| Forensic scientist | Approximate salary |
|---|---|
| Science technician | $32,275–$51,894 |
| Computer analyst | $53,565–$81,597 |
| Computer lab manager | $76,736–$118,042 |

Forensic examiners often have to find hidden or deleted files, and decipher encrypted or damaged information. The aim is to produce evidence that can be used to prosecute a suspected criminal in a court of law.

## Training and qualifications

45

For a career in computer forensics, you will need to study for a degree in computer forensics or have some experience working with a wide range of computer systems. Many certificate and degree programs are available, ranging from short courses for experienced computer scientists to university degree courses. A degree involves learning a combination of computer science and criminal justice. Relevant courses include those on computer hardware, software, networking, communications, and the internet. Also available are courses in criminal law, business studies, statistics, crime investigation, and the latest forensic techniques.

## Career prospects

An increasing number of criminals use computers and the internet to conduct their crimes, so the job outlook for computer forensic examiners is very good. In fact, there has never been such a good time to think about a career in computer forensics.

# Glossary

**bulletin board**—Web site that hosts messages and articles.

**chat room**—Web site where people can have discussions in real time by typing messages on their computer.

**convict**—To find a person guilty of a criminal charge.

**cyberterrorism**—Terrorist attacks against computers belonging to governments, banks, and other large organizations.

**data**—Organized information that may consist of numbers, words, or images.

**database**—A collection of information that is stored in a computer system.

**decipher**—To discover the meaning of something.

**digital**—Representing data as numbers.

**downloading**—Transferring a file from the internet onto a computer desktop.

**encrypted**—Converted into a secret code.

**firewalls**—Systems that protect computers from harm.

**fraud**—Deliberately misleading someone for personal gain.

**hacking**—Accessing computers without authorization from the owners.

**harassment**—Any threatening behavior used to frighten someone on a regular basis.

**identity theft**—Stealing personal details and using them to commit fraud.

**Internet**—A vast computer network that links smaller networks worldwide.

**launder**—To use the cash obtained from crime to buy legal goods and services.

**logic bombs**—Malicious programs that are triggered by an event, such as a date.

**malware**—Malicious software designed to damage computers.

**message boards**—Web pages on the internet that allow people to post messages and reply to the posts.

**peer-to-peer (P2P) networks**—Internet file-sharing networks.

**pharming**—A type of internet fraud in which hackers break into the computers that direct internet traffic.

**phishing**—A type of internet fraud in which people are tricked into disclosing personal information, such as bank account numbers.

**prosecute**—To charge with a crime.

**servers**—Computers that manage computer networks.

**spamming**—Sending bulk e-mail messages to advertise products or commit fraud.

**Trojan horses**—Malware that appears to be useful but secretly damages computer systems.

**viruses**—Malware that spreads from computer to computer, prompted by the computer user.

**worms**—Malware that spreads from computer to computer automatically.

**World Wide Web (www)**—All the information on the internet, which can be accessed using a browser.

**zombie network**—A vast computer network that is controlled by a hacker and used to send spam.

# Further reading

## Books

Bauchner, Elizabeth. *Computer Investigation*. Philadelphia: Mason Crest Publishers, 2006.

Dahl, Michael. *Computer Evidence*. Mankato, Minnesota: Capstone Press, 2007.

Day-Macleod, Deirdre. *Viruses and Spam*. New York: Rosen Central, 2008.

Newman, Matthew. *You Have Mail: True Stories of Cybercrime.* London: Franklin Watts, 2008.

## Web sites

Find out how forensic scientists use computers and virtual reality technology to map out crime scenes at:

**http://people.howstuffworks.com/vr-csi.htm**

Check out the Federal Bureau of Investigation web site:

**www.fbi.gov/cyberinvest/cyberhome.htm**

Learn about the qualifications and skills useful for a career in forensic science, and the range of jobs available, at:

**www.staysafeonline.org**

# Index

**48**